© 2013 by Curtis Hair

All rights reserved. No part of this work covered by the copyright herein may be reproduced, transmitted, stored, or used in any form or by any means graphic, electronic, or mechanical, including but not limited to photocopying, recording, scanning, digitizing, taping, web distribution, information networks, or information storage and retrieval systems, except as permitted under section 107 or 108 of the 1976 U.S. Copyright Act, without the written prior permission of the publisher.

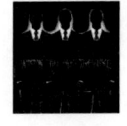

www.hairstonhandgun.com

Published by Hairston Handgun Firearms Training

Although the author and publisher have made every effort to ensure the accuracy and completeness of the information contained in this book, we assume no responsibility for errors, inaccuracies, omissions, or any inconsistency herein. Any similarities or assumptions of such by/to anyone represented in this body of work are unconfirmed and unintentional. Any slights of people, places, or organizations are unintentional.

ISBN: 978-0-9893500-3-7

First Printing: 2013

Printed in Canada

Editor: Evelyn Henry Miller

Interior Design: LaSonia Hairston

Cover Designer: JaaLisa Banks

Proofreader: David Mason

TABLE OF CONTENTS

Dedication	iii
Forward	iv
Introduction	v
CHAPTER ONE: THE PRINICIPAL	1
Learning Your Principal ^ EPO's Job Description ^ Making the Hard Decisions	
CHAPTER TWO: HOSPITALIZATION	8
Privacy ^ Advance Work ^ Confidentiality	
CHAPTER THREE: EXPOSURE CLOCK	13
Timing is Everything	
CHAPTER FOUR: TRAVEL WITH THE PRINICIPAL	16
Routes ^ Site Setup ^ Trip Preparation ^ Firearms	
CHAPTER FIVE: EMBARK/DEBARK	28
Planes ^ Trains ^ Automobiles ^ Hotels	
CHAPTER SIX: VENUE RULES AND SET-UP	34
Rules ^ Responsibility ^ Posture	
CHAPTER SEVEN: FORMATIONS	43
Rings of Protection ^ Assaults ^ The Force Continuum	
CHAPTER EIGHT: GUNS	50
Statistics ^ Rules of Deadly Force ^ Training ^ Carrying Weapons	
Summary	58
Appreciations	60
About the Author	61

<u>Dedication-</u>

First, I have to thank my Lord and Savior Jesus Christ for allowing me to exercise the gift He has given me to serve His people. It is not always that your gift and your passion line up and allow you to live life to the fullest. With that in mind, let me also thank my loving wife, LaSonia, for allowing me to flow and as I like to put it, "Do the Dang Thing." In this line of work, you have to have someone that can tolerate you keeping the secrets of your business--someone aware that you have to get up and go handle "situations" at a moment's notice. Thank you for loving me and encouraging me to always take it to the next level. Thank you to my parents. Thank you to my mother, who has stood for me even when I could not stand for myself. She has always been the inspiration for our family and many others. I love you, Momma! Thank you to my father, who supported his family and stayed and showed me what it means to be a real father to his children. Many, many thanks to my friend, my brother, my spiritual father, Bishop T.D. Jakes for trusting me enough to plant seed in my life, and stuck around to water it. You encourage me without fail. While serving and observing you, Sir, I have learned so much more about life, business and managing a family from a distance many times. The wisdom you imparted to me is invaluable, and it is with your blessing, Sir, that I share the gift that God has given me with others who share the same passion, and have the same call on their lives.

Forward-

While writing this Forward, CNN is covering the tragedy in Boston, during the Marathon. **Terror**, whether domestic or international, is still terror. In our day and age, we cannot have a "police state" in every public event we host. With that in mind, there is a need for men and women like Curtis Hairston, that have the unique training and competence to protect our churches, groups, and organizations.

Church has to be "open" so the Holy Spirit can flow. Concerts must be open so a connection can be made between performer and concert goers.
While these things are happening, who is watching?
Curtis Hairston and his staff ARE. **Curtis' book gives the reader basic tools and insight to help them secure and protect any client. You need to purchase and read this book, so you and your staff can be equipped to WATCH over others.**

Sean Smith

**-Lt. Sean Smith, Gwinnett County Sheriff's Dept.
April 2013**

Introduction-

The role of today's Executive Protection Officer (EPO) is primarily protecting the Principal from harm: physical, family and mind (peace of mind). Although being able to fight and defend yourself against a physical threat is required, for many Principals nowadays, there are more demands just as important to them that need addressing. Anything you can do to make their life easier counts. You will have to shield them from embarrassment, safeguard their schedules and visitors, and still thwart kidnappings, assassination attempts, and injuries. Your purpose is facilitating them to fulfill their purpose with little or no disturbances from outside sources. Whether they are a pastor, business executive, celebrity or spouse of a prominent person, the question remains: "Who is Watching While They Pray?" The answer should be the EPO. The reality is that it is probably someone else as well--someone who may intend to do harm. My hope is that these few words in this booklet will assist a new Executive Protection Officer to excel to the top of his game by providing that "little something extra" that gives him the edge. Also, I want to provide "old heads" like me a refresher course in some things we may have forgotten as we became comfortable. This is not for one-time reading. It is proactive reference material to keep you a step ahead of all the others who have been licensed to do what we do. This is not in any way proposed to be a complete list of "do's" and "don'ts," as you will find with more and more experience, but it could make the difference in having a onetime assignment as a bodyguard, or a permanent position as an Executive Protection Officer. Keep an open mind and digest what you need. Put the rest aside, but not too far away...you just may need it on a later date.

CHAPTER ONE - The Principal

<u>Learn YOUR Principal.</u> You will never find two that are exactly alike. "Let this mind be in you that is also in Christ Jesus." You cannot serve someone if you do not know their mind, their needs, desires and objectives. What is their vision? How they think and what's most important to them, etc. should also be most important to you. Watch them closely (but not while they are watching you, which can be a bit awkward). "Guarding Tess" is a movie that closely depicts the job of most of today's EPOs. You are not an adjutant, personal assistant, chief of staff or armor bearer, but your duties are somewhat the same at times and the lines will eventually cross. Do not be afraid to blur those lines. It will only make you more valuable, and many times, it is the chief of staff or assistant who is writing your check, not the Principal. The more you can take off their plate... the more valuable you become to them. You need to at least know these things about your Principal if you are, or are aspiring to be, their long term Personal/Executive Protection Officer:

1. Medications & health concerns or issues

2. Dietary preferences and exclusions

3. Food, drink and/or drug allergies

4. Blood type (and know yours as well)

5. Close family & friends (names, too)

6. Know all of the Principal's vehicles and the license plate numbers. It is good to log the expiration dates of inspection sticker, registration and insurance. Be sure the current insurance cards are available in each of their vehicles. You would not want any embarrassing moments with law enforcement if these items are not up to date and properly in place.

7. Develop an alias for the Principal, their spouse and any small

children. It should be a realistic name that will be used in professional situations. Let them know what it is. That is the name that will be changed on hotel registers after check-in, restaurant reservation at times, and anything else you can legally change on registrations and information sheets. Do not do an assumed name, business name or anything known or associated with them publicly that can be traced back to them. It can even be something funny or one they suggest to you. This is also a sacred name that will not be discussed publicly because, once it becomes common (and it will eventually), you will have to change it again. This is not the same code name that you and your team will use over radio communications to refer to the Principal and family. That one will be used for internal purposes only. And that one can be animated as necessary.

8. Know their favorite foods and drinks as well. How do they drink their tea, coffee, or alcohol? You may find yourself in a position that you have to order or even prepare their meals for them at times. That would be the time for you to suggest from what you already know they like, instead of having to read an entire menu to them. Also, it comes in handy in their holding "green room" at different venues, when hosts may ask what your Principal's desires are for setup purposes. It allows you to clear the room of additional host/hostesses when you already know what the Principal needs. You can relieve the host/hostess and you yourself become the host, if you have everything you need present. This means that a conversation should have taken place with the hosting team before your arrival (advance work) to discuss your Principal's desires.

9. Remember, you have no lane to stay in when it comes to your Principal. You will wear many hats and do many jobs if you want longevity. Watch everyone around him and what they bring to the table in reference to his well-being and daily activities. Notice what the Principal's like and dislikes are. Take a mental note on everything said and done. It is not unusual for them to

get off a phone call and ask you for the number that someone just gave them. Even though they did not ask you, they were expecting you to note it or write it down since they repeated it aloud. I am not saying eavesdrop...or am I? Hmmmm... My wife says I am nosey. In this business, we call it being "aware of your surroundings." When you hear a conversation about your client having a headache, why would you not be "Johnny on the Spot" and have some aspirin ready when they got off the call? They will at least know that you are paying attention to detail. And that is a must.

10. You should always be "the bad guy" when it comes to unwanted or awkward public encounters, when it is time to leave a venue or PR session, or when fan photos need to cease. You politely, but aggressively, end the session by escorting your Principal away. You can remind them about that important situation that needs their attention in just a few minutes...hint, hint. The Principal may resist a bit at first until they trust your judgment (which comes with more history). You can still have a pleasant disposition and aggressively keep your Principal moving along. You also have to be the judge of when a photo session or PR session becomes dangerous or embarrassing for your Principal.

For example:

Just a while ago, I was on a detail in a foreign country on the way to promote an event at a radio station and to offer tickets to an event featuring the Principal. The police motorcade escorted our vehicle into a busy downtown area that ended with a dead end. As other vehicles turned in behind us, there was no longer a "legitimate" exit, per se. Because the crowd was thickening, the promoter had a bright idea that the Principal should open the sun roof on our vehicle and wave to the crowd and maybe pass out some tickets to the event. I immediately declined the request, but the Principal pleaded for me to allow it. I repeatedly argued against it, stating that the crowd was unstable, had not been screened, and it was dangerous to do so without better positioning of the vehicle and protection staff. After further denial to the promoter from me, he decided to hand out the free tickets himself next to our vehicle. The crowd rushed the promoter and knocked him onto the hood of our vehicle and began rocking our car as well, while mobbing the promoter for the show tickets. I told the driver to begin driving and honking the horn through the crowd. After some hesitation and further intense encouragement from me that if he did not drive, I would remove him from the vehicle and drive myself, we began moving and maneuvering up onto the curb in front of us. The police escort finally got the notion to drive up over the curb as well, allowing for an alternate exit. As we maneuvered through the crowd, I politely asked the Principal if he would still like for me to stop and allow him to exit the vehicle to give away the tickets. Although I do not recommend commenting like that, there may be a time when you have to remind the Principal of why they are paying you. It is not just about following instructions and obeying the client's wishes. Many times, it is about having the courage and professional insight to tell the Principal, "No." Just be sure when and if you ever do, that you are confident in your decision. And, be able to articulate to the Principal why you are recommending such action.

In another situation, again overseas, I found myself with my principal in an armored vehicle, headed to a venue where he was to speak. Two blocks from the venue, he turned to me and said that he had to relieve himself immediately. This was a problem because, although we were two blocks away from the venue, we were in "stop and go" traffic. We could already see the people waiting outside, stretched around the building in which he was to speak. The Principal said, "Well let's get out and walk to one of these stores because someone will let me in." I immediately said, "No Sir. That is not a good idea at all because the crowd is too thick. We don't know this crowd, and we are already in an armored vehicle, so let's stay here and ride it out. Also, these store owners may not let you in to relieve yourself." While I was yet talking, he opened his door and jumped out saying, "We have to find a place, now." Now remember, we were in a foreign country and do not speak the language. So, as we ran from storefront to storefront, discovering that a "go away" hand gesture and a frown from the local store owners mean the same thing in every language, he realized that I was correct in my assumption. While pulling his hat down to cover his face, he then decided we must make our way through the crowd outside to get to the inside of the venue, since we no longer had our vehicle. As we pushed our way to what we thought was the front of the line, someone recognized him. While 1,000 people began pressing their way towards us, the Principal exclaims, "This was not a good idea! This is not safe for us!" I replied, "No, Sir, it was not and it is not, but it is too late to turn back now. I will cover you the best I can, so let's try to move, we cannot stand still. The only way through is to press towards the tall gate ahead and we can enter through there." After 15 minutes of plowing through the crowd, with the crowd pulling and tearing at his clothing, we made it to the gate, which was still another 25 yards from what we believed to be the entrance. I hoisted the Principal up about 6 feet, which was halfway up the gate. I held his ankle as I continued to press through the crowd below him, with people pulling and tugging at his clothing. Meanwhile, I was getting beaten on my chest, back, and legs while holding his ankle with one hand and throwing elbows with the other. When I could go no further because the crowd had obstructed my movements, I instructed the Principal to climb the remainder of the gate, which was about 6 additional feet above him and jump over to the other side to safety. Once he was secure on the other side, I pressed on for about 15 more minutes continuing towards the gate entrance. Upon arrival to what we had hoped was the gate entrance, I realized that none of the security on the other side of the gate spoke English. I also realized that this was not an entrance at all; it was the rear of the venue, so the gate was locked. I could see the assistant and team members scanning the crowd looking for me, which I figured they were doing because the Principal had made it to safety and told them of my demise, but they could not hear me over the screams of the crowd surrounding me. The rowdy crowd continued pushing towards the gate, and I observed others around me being crushed against the gate screaming. Once my face touched the gate, I immediately began discharging my stun gun on the lower extremities of those pressing against me. No one could hear it because of the noisy crowd. I suddenly had more breathing room. I stretched out my elbows to the gate so that I would not be crushed overseas. Finally, the Principal's assistant spotted me and grabbed a translator, saying, "Get him out of there!" After about 10 more minutes of chaos, someone finally found a maintenance man with keys. He unlocked the gate and allowed me, and about 20 others who forced their way in, to enter. When I finally made it inside, I realized that the crowd outside was not people standing in line. It consisted of individuals who could not get in because the venue was full, so they really had no urgency of letting us make it through to get inside. The Principal sincerely and deeply apologized for putting us in that situation. I responded that my purpose when we travel is to get ALL of us home safely, not just him, and in the future he has to trust and adhere to my instructions concerning our safety. He agreed that this would not happen again.

You are the security and safety professional. The Principal is paying you to protect them. It may be uncomfortable at first telling your boss what to do and what not to do, but as soon as you get caught up in a situation because you did not open your mouth, you will learn quickly to speak up. Be professional, tactful, and direct in situations that call for it. It could mean the difference between life or death--yours and theirs. Hurt feelings will heal. And they will understand it better by and by. There was no option in the middle of those crowds to panic and shut down. The Principal was in trouble. It did not matter how we got there. It was The EPO's job to get us out with little or no harm to the Principal. My statement to my wife when I leave the house for an overseas assignment is always, "I will be coming home the same as when I left." On that last trip I returned a bit bruised up...but I returned and the Principal did as well.

NOTES:

CHAPTER TWO - Hospitalization

Should you ever have the unfortunate event of hospitalization for the Principal or their spouse, there are some procedures that help facilitate a media-free transition.

1. First and foremost, limit the people who know of the event until they are released and back securely. And even then, that information will not come from you. It will be from whomever they designate to disseminate that information to the pubic (PR, publicist, Chief of Communications). Just because they have additional family members does not mean they all need to know, or even be there for the hospitalization event.

2. Run the route yourself and figure out the best way to get to the hospital at that particular time of day, if at all possible. You should already know the closest and most exclusive hospital to the client's workplace and home. And the closest may not necessarily be the nicest, but you need them both.

3. Contact the hospital and ask to speak to the charge nurse. Let her know that you have a VIP that will be having a procedure at their location and you want anonymity and to keep their name off all of their public lists. While on this subject, do not list your Principal's real name in your cell phone. Come up with another name or alias if you have not already. The hospital has procedures in place for your Principal. Your VIP is not their first, so let them do their job; however, it is your job to be sure it was done properly before the day of the procedure, if at all possible. The charge nurse will probably get you in touch with the head of security at the hospital as well. Introduce yourself as "Your Name" the Executive Protection Officer for a high profile individual who will be having a procedure in your hospital (keep in mind that you will probably have to go ahead and name drop at this point to insure total cooperation).

Be as polite and courteous as possible in your requests. Let them know how much you and the Principal appreciate all of their assistance in taking care of them or their family. Ask if you can meet with them (charge nurse and security supervisor) if you have time. This would be a good time to check the parking situation. Ask the security supervisor for favors like parking in their spot or another close, secure or secluded entrance. Be sure and get their business card. You may have to flash it or refer to it on procedure day when you are questioned about what you are doing. Do not volunteer the information that you will be armed; however, if the Security Supervisor asks, your answer should be with confidence, "Yes...I am working." While I am on that subject...that is the answer for any law enforcement who asks that question as well. You are not being a smarty; you are just affirming to them that you are working. If they question further, just show them your credentials (which should ALWAYS be with you) and let them know you have a client. Remember, you are in their house and you want to have anything in the way of "special favors" you can get to help please your Principal and make them as comfortable as possible. So, it is a great idea to "humbly" make your request known to the security supervisor. Then you can usually expect professional courtesy in return.

4. Know how many people are expected to wait for the Principal/spouse and check on waiting areas available in that area. Private waiting areas work best, but may not be readily available, but again I say...ASK for it. You never know what they can work out for your Principal. Remember, they are not doing it for you, so keep your Principal's name in your mouth when asking for favors from the individuals who can make things happen. It may open doors that are normally closed to normal people like you and me. There have been occasions when the hospital gave a private patient room across the hall at no charge and filled it with meals, snacks and drinks for the waiting family. There is no telling how far they will go to please your Principal. Anything that makes them more comfortable in this stressful time of family illness is greatly welcomed and appreciated. It

is always a good point, afterwards, to have someone from the Principal's office to send a card, flowers or something special to those staff members at the hospital who made your stay much more pleasant. A letter of appreciation to their boss does not hurt, either. This also paves the way for further visits from other family members or the Principal themselves. As always, gather business cards and document names and numbers for assistance in the future if needed.

5. Depending on the circumstances, you may want to post outside of their hospital room door and monitor traffic. In any case, you should at least be in the closest waiting area, but be where you can monitor anyone attempting to visit their room. Unfortunately, media and others can pose as hospital staff and enter at will if unchallenged. Check the hospital board for the names of the staff that will be servicing your client and monitor who enters the room. Request that the same nurse and caretakers are used for the duration of your stay. Ask for a chair to sit outside of the room if this is an all-night detail. If you change shift with another EPO, be sure to brief them on all activity and what to expect. This hospital assignment should be kept very close to the vest. It should not be information that you release to anyone, not even for the company you work for unless totally necessary for you to do the job. I have released personal protection officers for divulging personal information about their client--even to me. If I cannot assist you in any way with the assignment, what you are telling me only becomes gossip. There is no use for an EPO who gossips. No matter how in demand the information is that you have concerning your client. Respect your profession and have the integrity to take that information to your grave, not theirs. You should continue to protect their privacy, even when they are no longer with us. And I mean that one! If you violate that trust, you are ending your career publicly. Who will ever trust you again? Who would hire you?

This brings me to my next point:

What you see, what you hear, what the Principal/spouse did, who visited, who called, where they went, who they visited, when they will be in/out of town (I think you get it), should NEVER be repeated by you or your staff at any time. All you have in this business is your character. That cannot be taught or read in a book (pun intended). That will be the difference between you and someone else, maybe even less qualified, in your position. Your Principal's business should not be used for bragging rights or pillow talk. Your spouse should not know "exactly" how your day went. That is unacceptable on so many levels. Hopefully, you signed a confidentiality agreement. If not, you should create one, have an attorney review it, and sign it yourself. And you should also make sure that anyone in close contact with your Principal has signed one as well. For example, consider the following: personal trainers, housekeepers, hair stylists or barbers, make-up artists, landscapers, maintenance workers, window washers and anyone coming to perform any repairs around the home, all contractors and any of your people that will be assisting you with your Principal. Their assistants and office workers and definitely anyone traveling with them should sign a non-disclosure (confidentiality) statement. It may be awkward at times to get people to sign, but when you briefly explain that it is for the Principal's protection, they usually submit and sign it. If they do not, deny them access and immediately let your Principal know. He may need to intervene to override it or dismiss them from having access. This will usually not apply to personal friends as they are probably VIP's themselves. When in doubt...ALWAYS ask the Principal before embarrassing them or their friends by asking them to sign one. That is a great point to remember...ALWAYS ask if you are unsure of what is required or what the Principal wants. Also, if in doubt, err on the side of caution. I am not saying to stay in their face, constantly bothering them with issues that you should be resolving. Remember, it is your responsibility to keep things off of their plate. Protection of their mind, body and overall well-being is your job. But, you should be mindful and aware of your "Exposure Clock."

NOTES:

CHAPTER THREE - Exposure Clock

Time spent in your Principal's presence is important. It will eventually run out if you don't manage it properly. Your Principal sees a lot of you, sometimes morning, noon and night. Sometimes they spend more time with you than with their spouse. It is not your fault. You are needed; however, when you get a chance to NOT be in their face...it would be wise to do just that. Many times they are with you more than with their spouse. As much as they need you, want you, and even sometimes love you, they will eventually get tired of seeing your face all day, every day. You can usually tell when this is happening, and my advice to you is to disappear, but don't go too far. Always be where they can get to you if needed, but usually when they are at this point, they probably won't need you anytime soon. Oh, yes, and please do not take it personally. Of course, you want to feel like one of the family or at least a good friend and confidant, but always remember...you are hired help as well. Even when you are not working...you are working. Yes, you can wind down and enjoy the moment if you are pulled in to do so by them, but never forget your place or get too comfortable and common with the Principal/spouse and/or their family or friends. That is a trap, not intentionally set by anyone, but it hurts the same when you come to yourself or they have to remind you of your place.

A Principal recently told me that my mentor and I are the only EPOs he has worked with that give him his space, and we know how to be a friend and a professional at the same time. He said that one previous EPO had gotten so common with him that he thought it would be alright to ask him to borrow money...incredible! The Principal gave him the money, and he soon after replaced him.

Also, do not get caught up into being your Principal's "yes man." They can get that anywhere from anyone trying to use them for gain or to suck up to them for whatever reason. They look to you for the educated truth as you know it. You are their "Minister of Information." Your job is to speak honestly and intelligently with tactfulness, integrity and courage--to say and do what is right for the circumstances of the moment. And remember, whatever you decide to do...own it. There is nothing worse than a person in leadership making excuses or blaming someone else for their actions. Take the fall if you get tripped up. Get up quickly. Shake yourself off and get back to work. Your job is far too important for you to sit around and wallow in your mess and mistakes, licking your wounds. How you recover after a mishap makes ALL the difference. My grandmother used to say, "Everybody booboo's, but just don't booboo and fall back in it. Keep stepping forward." Have a conversation with the Principal and acknowledge that you get it and take ownership of the error you made. "I dropped the ball!" is a hard thing to say, but that is how you move forward. And they need to understand why you erred, so they know it won't happen again. FIX the problem; apologize if warranted; assure them that "this" will not happen again, and then quickly get on with the business at hand. Again, you are too important to sit on the sidelines. Get back in the game!

NOTES:

CHAPTER FOUR - Travel with the Principal

When you think of travel, don't just think about travel on a plane or even out of town. The same rules apply whenever you are away from your normal surroundings at home (U.S.). These basic rules are even more important when in unfamiliar territory, like foreign countries or even during domestic travel. I have travelled with a Principal to forty-one different countries in the past eight years, so trust me when I say, "It is good to have a 'system' in place." One caveat, we are referred to as "ugly Americans" in some other countries because of our unwillingness to adjust and adapt to the surroundings we are placed in. Instead we "get an attitude" or arrogance about us and expect things to be like they are at home (food, accommodations, drink, sanitation, hygiene, service, etc.). Please do not embarrass your Principal or your country by reinforcing the stereotype. And, be sure you inform the Principal of what is acceptable or disrespectful in these countries. There are other ways of expressing your disinterest in eating the squid heads, caviar, spicy eel, goat head soup, shark fin or other delicacy that has been placed before you. Turning up your nose and expressions like, "Ewww," and, "What the...?" or, "Oh, H.... No!" would be disrespectful in any language. And, if it is a formal meal, your hosts are usually waiting, with baited breath, for your expression to ensure they have pleased you with their ultimate selection. Sometimes you have to just grin and bear it and take one for the country. It all comes out in the end...literally.

Surveying Your Route:

Your survey should note any areas that could present a problem for your travel. Have a primary and secondary route. Pay close attention to all overpasses and construction areas. Make note of possible choke points that may impede traffic or bring you to a stop. Use maps and GPS when possible to ensure directions are clear and simple to follow. Always get the drivers' names and phone numbers before their arrival, and if not, get them immediately upon pick up. Check and evaluate all emergency data and communications equipment.

Surveying the Site (Advance):

The purpose of the site survey is to identify undesirable elements and physical hazards that may interfere with your visit. It is more advantageous to do a site visit before you arrive with the Principal. Unfortunately, you may not have that luxury. If you arrive with the Principal, get them settled and secure in their holding (green) room and immediately begin your site survey. Your first plan of action would be to contact the person in charge of the site (Production Mgr., Security Director, Pastor's Assistant, etc.) and ask for a quick walkthrough of your route to the stage or venue. Examine all factors that may be difficult to control. Check and evaluate all emergency data and communications equipment again. Note the crowd location and buffer zones. View onlookers and scan the crowd for anyone looking strange or even uninterested in the event. Ask about any in-house security assistance that may be available and their post locations. Get the cell numbers of all individuals who may be assigned to your team as additional security escorts. Investigate and determine the adequacy of the emergency escape route.

Some basic guidelines for foreign travel:

1. Always register your team and the Principal with The U.S. State Department at www.travel.state.gov or www.usembassy.gov. Although you will normally keep all of this information very "close to the vest," it is advisable to give The State Department the information they are requesting so that they may assist you abroad if needed. If no one knows where to start looking for you, it would make it much more difficult to find you in an emergency. They would also be the one trying to contact you, should something go wrong in the country you are visiting, that may adversely affect your safety or travel. You will want to do this for every overseas trip. You will need the phone number for the Regional Security Officer (RSO) for the country you are visiting. Get the number and address of the closest U.S. Embassy. The number for the nearest Marine post can be found there as well, if available. Again, if an unfortunate situation should arise while abroad, these numbers can facilitate assistance in getting you and your team to safety. I have had the unfortunate opportunity to test its effectiveness while in Uganda right in the middle of a riot that had erupted. And, for the record, THE SYSTEM WORKS! If it had failed me...there would be no *Who is Watching While They Pray* authored by me. After finding a somewhat safe place to hunker down for about seven hours, we were escorted to safety by the country's military. If the proper arrangements and advance work had not been done prior to the trip, no one would or could have known who was with me, why we were there, or even where to start looking for the fifteen Americans abroad in the middle of a volatile upris-

ing. DO THE WORK! Register your trip with The U.S. State Department. It will someday show its value to you. There is also a convenient app to The U.S. State Department for your smart phone or tablet called "Smart Traveler." The app has a wealth of information and you can actually securely register and update your team's travel from there.

2. When in a crowd of unknowns, always stay no further than an arm's length away. If you are carrying a weapon, get in the habit of keeping your client opposite your weapon side. This will allow you to move him out of the way with one hand and obtain your weapon simultaneously with the other hand, should that day ever come.

3. Always carry antibacterial instant soap and small mints in your pocket. If the Principal is a celebrity or well known, you never know when a close-talker wants a private conversation with the Principal. A small mint can usually keep them prepared. They may also shake a lot of hands and sit down to eat or already be seated. Always be discreet with the soap; however, you do not want it to look like they are trying to wash the "people's" dirt off them. If you do not have the opportunity to do it discreetly, then do not do it at all. But the bottom line, again, is you are protecting him from potential illness. I recently had an officer who was "under the weather" to board a private plane with the Principal. When asked by the Principal if he was sick, he replied, "No...I'll be fine." After several hours of hacking and coughing, we arrived to our destination. The Principal turned to him and said, "You should have stayed at home." He again replied, "I'm not that bad, I'll be fine." Upon arrival to the hotel, and after pleading his case on why he wanted to stay and serve his Principal, I brought to his attention that it was not about him... it was about him infecting all of us while he was flying around on a private plane, breathing the same air for hours. Of course, I sent him home on the first available plane to get healed. Unfortunately, the Principal awoke the next day deathly ill, and my

officer and I looked very irresponsible and inconsiderate for not leaving that officer behind from the beginning. It is YOUR job to protect your client from ANYTHING or ANYONE who might hinder the Principal from completing their mission, even if that anyone means you. Never forget that their vision or objective is bigger than you. And, it is never about you. Don't take it personally. Do whatever you have to do to keep them safe, even if it means you have to bow out for a minute and get a viable replacement. This also means that you should have a viable, trained replacement handy in case of emergencies.

4. Carry additional items in your "go bag" to take on the plane. Items like Jell-O, protein bars, pudding, trail mix, nuts, and dried fruit go a long way on long flights. Include a first aid kit in that "go bag," but be mindful of plane regulations and restrictions. Plus, you never know when you or your Principal might get the munchies, while hunkered down for seven hours with fifteen Americans you are responsible for, abroad, waiting on the military to come and assist you in getting out of a country in the middle of a rebel uprising...Hmmmm. Furthermore, you never know when you have to hit the ground running without time for a meal. But again, remember, everything is not allowable for carry-on luggage. With that in mind, a nice "511" backpack comes in real handy for a "go bag" when you have to carry a couple pieces of luggage for the Principal. I had to retire my 15 inch laptop and laptop roller bag and just load up my iPad in my "go bag." The Principal is not usually concerned with what you brought along to carry (even though it may be for them). They do want to be sure, though, that you have room enough and hands available for all their stuff. So be prepared for their items, and make sure yours is easy to manage. You will only make the mistake once of looking like a pack mule, then you will size down your personal travel packages.

5. Make it a point to treat your Principal with the same respect and courtesy you would give a woman in a relationship when it

comes to how you care for them, whether they are female or not--and whether you are female or not. That makes it easier to remember in a "what should I do" situation. To clarify, open all doors for them (cars, buildings, elevators) and assist them if necessary. Help them with their coats and hats. Carry items for them (meaning, you cannot have a lot of your stuff to carry in the way). If you find yourself with your hands full, it is time for you to assist them in picking out a small bag in which you can carry their things. Slide your seat up in the car if sitting in front of them (which you should). It is not about your comfort. It is always about theirs. I am not saying to put your knees in your chest, but definitely give them as much leg room as you can spare. Ask them if they have enough room and if they are comfortable with the seat position and air temperature. Quickly turn the radio off when entering the car of a driver that is transporting you and your Principal. Ask the Principal if he wants the radio, if so, then turn it back on, but do not take it for granted or let the driver do so either.

6. When questions are asked about your Principal by anyone, including the people who may have invited you to the event and are paying for it, be sure to deflect the question. What I am saying is to not be rude, but sometimes it is good to just look at them and say nothing. If in the presence of the Principal, pause long enough to let him answer if he wants. Nothing is wrong in saying, "We don't discuss that," or "Well, we don't talk about things like that," or even, "And, why do you need to know that again?" Those answers usually make the person asking the question feel uncomfortable with pursuing that line of questioning further. You MUST at all times keep the smallest bit of information about your client concealed. What you may deem to be a small issue could very well end up being your last day in that position due to your lack of confidentiality. If anyone ever asks you for their contact information, even in the Principal's presence, always give them your information. That includes phone number, email address, etc. It is good to immediately get

some business cards made so that it does not take up too much of your time to give them what they are requesting. Never give out the Principal's information--again, not even to their friends. You never want to end up being the source of any leak. KEEP YOUR MOUTH SHUT!! The less you say, the better you and your Principal are protected. There is nothing wrong with a simple, "I don't know." Bail out!!!

7. When traveling with your firearm there are some points to remember:

>A. You will need a hard sided, lockable container that securely holds the weapon in place. You can use an external lock or a container that has one built in.

>B. You will need a suitcase (can be the one you are already packing for checked baggage, but leave room for your hard sided lockable container).

>C. You need to purchase a TSA approved lock for your suitcase. This lock will have the TSA logo on it and say that it is TSA approved. That means a TSA officer can unlock it with their approved key if necessary to check inside.

>D. The magazine must be removed from the firearm and emptied. The chamber must be locked back on the firearm to the open position for viewing that it is empty. If it does not lock open, place a cable lock in it to keep it opened.

>E. The empty magazines have no particular placing required. I would, however, be sure they are at least somewhere in the same suitcase where the firearm is for accessibility.

F. The ammunition must be in the box it came in (it does not have to be this brand in the same name brand box, though). Some airlines will allow you to place the box of ammo in with your firearm; others will not. So, just place that box somewhere secure in the same suitcase as your hard sided lockable container.

G. Close the box, but do not lock it yet. You will need to go into at the airport and possibly confirm with the ticket processor that the firearm is unloaded.

H. Place the box in the suitcase with the TSA lock on it and head to the airport.

I. You cannot curbside check-in while checking a firearm.

You must go inside to a ticket agent and ask for a "declaration." Each airport has their own form, but they all basically say the same thing. "I declare, as required by federal air regulations, that the firearm being checked as baggage is unloaded." If the ticket agent asks you what you are talking about, tell them you need a declaration to check your firearm. Do not use the word "gun" in the airport. There are two types of declarations for firearms. If they ask you, you want the one that allows you to check it with your luggage, not the one to carry on the plane on your person. That would be a felony in process and would probably ruin your plans for the evening, or the next few years. Sign the declaration, date it, and put it on top of the firearm container. Someone will tape it to the container; others will just require that it is in the suitcase with the container.

J. Some airlines will also ask to see that the weapon is unloaded. If so, unlock your suitcase and turn it towards them. Open the firearm container and turn it towards them. DO NOT HANDLE THE WEAPON IN THE AIRPORT unless they ask you to turn it for them to see. In that case, lift it slightly and put it back down.

K. Close the hard sided lockable container and secure it this time. Place the declaration in the suitcase as required and lock the suitcase with the TSA lock.

L. The ticket agent will give you your ticket and identification and call for a TSA to escort you to another area for inspection from TSA. This may be the oversized baggage area or another screening area set aside for special circumstances. TSA will use their key to open your suitcase. They will inspect that the bag is properly packed and labeled accordingly with the declaration. They will place a sticker or tag inside stating that they have inspected it and tell you they have finished. Your suitcase, along with your contents will show up in baggage claim with all other passengers. No other special requirements.

8. Your clothing overseas should never look military. It is never a bad idea to have a suit handy. It is also classy in any language to wear a nice suit, or at least a jacket. Suits are universal and can be worn anytime of the day or night. A suit is also good to conceal whether you are carrying a weapon or not. It is never a good idea to expose that you are not carrying a weapon. Always keep them guessing and assuming that you have "something." Avoid Army green and camouflage clothing while abroad. Cargo pants are nice because they are comfortable and have several pockets for your Principal's stuff if needed. A nice "511" black or tan vest would also be a good recommendation. Boots are alright to wear, but make them low-quarter. A good, leather lace up shoe with rubber soles is always welcomed. Just a side note: lace up shoes should be the norm for any detail assignment and double tie the laces securely. Slip-on shoes are

not recommended. Keep a baseball style cap and sunglasses handy for extremely sunny conditions.

In reference to the items listed above under "4," here is another break down of the minimum items to carry in your "go bag" while traveling. Keep in mind, again, some of these would have been packed in checked baggage:

-First Aid Kit with Trauma Kit and AED if able

-Mosquito spray with Deet

-Medicine Variety packs: Airborne (keeps your immune system up), pain medicine, aspirin, diarrhea medicine, stool softener, No-Doze, Sleep Ease, 5-hour Energy, Claritin, Tums, cold remedies, Dramamine for car/plane sickness and papaya enzymes for upset stomachs.

-Jell-O and protein bars or meal replacement bars, trail mix (keep in mind if anyone has a peanut allergy to avoid certain foods)

-Phone chargers, back-up battery and accessories with all foreign country adapters. Be sure you have additional phone chargers and cords for the Principal as well. You may have to give up yours if they forgot theirs. So be aware of the model and type of cell phone and tablet they use.

-Extra flashlight or two

-Anti-bacterial soap (you can never have too many small bottles)

-Baby wipes and toilet tissue (you will never know the value until you need it, and don't have it)

-An extra pair of underwear, pants and a shirt is a nice asset to have in case of an unexpected spill, or something else.

-Spare glasses, if you wear contacts, and extra contacts

-Small, collapsible umbrella

-**Copies of ALL passports** of your travel team (you should request these from everyone before your trip). It is also good for someone else in the party to have copies as well. They will be very helpful in lost or stolen passport situations.

NOTES:

_____

_____

_____

_____

_____

_____

_____

_____

_____

_____

_____

_____

_____

_____

NOTES:

CHAPTER FIVE - Embark/Debark Vehicle and/or Plane

On a commercial flight, it is best to sit next to your Principal to keep others from disturbing him. But remember, it is always best to ask this question once to see what his/her take is on that. On a private plane, you are better positioned behind him, so you can see if he needs something by his gestures, etc. Remember though, on a private plane, you need to get off in front of him. Assist him if necessary. Immediately upon landing, check on your driver(s) to ensure they are in place. Of course, that also means that you checked on them before takeoff as well.

In a vehicle, always take the front passenger seat. Seat the Principal directly behind you. Let the driver know that you will take care of the Principal's door (open and close). Although usually against the law, I sometimes buckle the seatbelt behind me to allow me a quick exit to maneuver if necessary. Do not allow the driver to control the atmosphere. Turn the radio down immediately, unless you know your Principal wants it otherwise. By the time you ask the driver to do it, and he finally understands what you are saying, the Principal can already be irritated by the radio, so do it quickly yourself. Ask the Principal about the temperature in the vehicle. And, YOU adjust it if needed. Do not let the driver startup conversations with your Principal unless you know it is warranted. A slight gesture or touch to let the driver know to shut it up is usually enough. If your client is on a private phone call, you may want to turn the radio on at a low volume to distract the driver from listening to the conversation. You may also want to confirm the distance with the driver after you begin on your way as well. Remember, you should have already done this during your advance, but you should "confirm" it within earshot of your client to keep them from asking you. Always be sure that information relayed to the Principle is accurate and verified, or be sure to let them know that it is not verified when you relay the information. There is nothing worse than passing on a rumor or unverified information and having your Principle pass it on to someone else. That may get you dismissed.

Again, always carry instant antibacterial soap (even locally). Your Principal may shake many hands during an entrance to dinner or an exit. You never know where their hands have been (protection). But, be very discreet with the soap if you are still in the people's presence. It may appear to be rude if you squirt their hands down immediately after shaking someone's hand.

<u>Travel Procedures:</u> "ADVANCE" if at all possible, gather all drivers (name, phone#, type of vehicle), venue and address and security contact if available, hotel information and distances to and from the venues and airport. This was discussed in detail in "Chapter Four – Travel With The Principal."

Note the nearest hospitals, nice restaurants, hotel security name and number. I have over 5,700 contacts in my cell phone, but maybe 200 are personal contacts. Information and relationships will take you farther in this field than you could believe. You want to be the "go to" person in time of need. It only makes you more valuable. When the Principal thinks of you, they will think of you and everything else you bring to the table. Your wisdom, street smarts, intelligence, information, will to succeed, and your contacts and relationships elsewhere will all be considered when they call upon you for an assignment.

Airport:

If flying private, always call the pilot (you should have their number) to let them know that you are on the way and give them an estimated time of arrival (ETA). Note somewhere what the tail number is for the private plane. It is possible you will need it again for airport entry or something else. If flying commercial, check and double check the gate information for drop off and pick up of you and the Principal. You need an average time and a final time that they can arrive to the airport and still make the flight. You need to give them both times. It is good to create some sort of recognizable unique bag tags for your entire party for commercial travel. A picture or sample of this can be given to whoever is assisting with luggage in the baggage claim area. Always be sure that you or your designee has accounted for ALL luggage before leaving the airport. Check your luggage with the Principal's luggage at the ticket counter. They probably will have higher status than you on the airline and will get preferential treatment with their bags. Your bags need to stay together since you will always move with them. When going through TSA screening, you go in front of them so that you can assist them on the other side after quickly getting yourself together.

Hotel to Venue:

Call the hotel with your reservation number and let them know your ETA. Ask if they can pull your room keys and have them ready for a quick check-in. The least amount of time your Principal spends in the lobby, the better. Even if only their room is ready, that's OK. Get them situated and come back for yours. Come back to the hotel registration and change your Principal's name listed on his room to an alias that you have previously discussed with him. Be sure he knows in case he wants someone to call him in his room. He will need to give them the name. This "alias" name should be kept close to the vest and discussed only with key personnel involved in his travel. It should NOT be discussed with the person who is probably paying for the room (whomever invited him to speak, etc.). Also, neither they nor their host/hostess, if any, need to ever escort him to his room upon arrival. Have them wait in the lobby and you can go back to confirm that everything is fine if need be (take control of the situation). You have to set a precedence from the beginning that you are ultimately responsible for his well-being even though they think they are.

Hotel to Restaurants:

Make a list of the ones your Principal may like. Verify them with the locals or the hotel that they would meet his standards, whether it is upscale or down home. Call the restaurant before visiting and speak with the manager. Let them know you have a VIP guest and would like private seating if available and for how many in your party (guesstimate and add four -- always). Request a private or quiet section of the restaurant if available. Request that the adjoining tables are only used for seating if they have no other choices. You may not get everything requested, but as always...ask for it.

Luggage/Bags:

You assist with carrying luggage if no assistance is available. This means you need to practice at home carrying additional baggage while still being able to get to your weapon(s) or maneuver if required. That last thing you want to be is tied down with baggage when a situation arises. Assist all the way to the Principal's seat on the plane, and then take your seat. You board when they board, even if you are not in the same class of service. Always just say, "I'm working," if asked by airline staff questions like, "Where are you going?" (when you don't have a first class ticket). Or, "I have to get my client situated." They always understand. But again, remember that a smile and polite approach will get you much grace under situations as this.

Walking Movements:

Walk behind and to one side of the Principal, not more than an arm's length away, so you can see them and any danger, fans, etc. that may become an issue. Remember, your weapon side (reaction side) should be away from the Principal. Also, this avoids your face being in all of the camera shots, if present. Most Principals do not want the impression that they need a body guard everywhere they go. So, avoid the camera if at all possible. Sometimes that means you will have to give up a little of your comfort zone to allow for a better camera shot for PR purposes. Always keep your "weapon side" free from obstacles, if able. Keep the Principal on the other side in front of you. There should be a host or venue personnel escorting up front. If not, you may have to take the lead and keep aware of what is behind your Principal at the same time. When you are clear and can reposition yourself again behind them, it is advisable to do so. You do not want your Principal trying to find his way backstage or to the restroom, etc. You should always map that out for them. Even if you are behind them say, "Make a right / left here, a few more steps up here," and so on.

Checking Hotel Rooms:

"Sweep" the rooms quickly by checking at least the closets, shower and under the bed and behind curtains. Assist them in setting up the room if needed (laptop, cell phone on charger etc.) and write down the room numbers of you, and anyone traveling with them, on a piece of paper; ask if everything is fine, or anything else is needed, then leave. Remember your "Exposure Clock." Remember to do a quick run-through if able, upon checkout as well. There is nothing like having to turn around and leave the Principal because they left a package, cell phone, bag or something else in their room and you did not sweep it and check the room's safe box. Now you have to leave them, uncovered in most cases, to go back to the room and do what should have been done before. It can take less than a minute the first time. They would usually appreciate it and wait for you to do it anyway when they see you taking an interest.

NOTES:

_____

_____

_____

_____

_____

_____

_____

_____

_____

_____

_____

_____

CHAPTER SIX - Venue Rules and Setup

Request to talk to venue security (if possible); otherwise, you have to quickly try to implement on "show day" after you get your Principal secure at the venue. Or, try to get a driver to take you to the venue if time allows, once you get your Principal settled at their hotel.

You would like at least 20 feet or more between the stage area and the first set of chairs at an indoor venue. Outside, barriers work best, if able. Always request to have barriers (bicycle racks) on any outdoor venue. Thirty feet or more is a good distance between the barrier and the stage of an outdoor venue. They will probably not want to give up more than that. If you get it, great! If not, at least you asked for it (in case something goes wrong).

Request in-house assistance if available. And if they are available, walk through YOUR procedures with their security lead or the group, if able. Again, if not available then you are on your own. Let their security team know that you have 3 rules at your functions...

1. "If they get on the barrier... please make them get down."
2. "If they come over the barrier... put them on the ground."
3. "If they make it on stage with me... they get a beat down!" (from me).

In foreign countries, it is best to utilize their local security guys as the first couple levels of security, whether it is police or in house security. It is always a better look for them to handle their own, especially physically; however, you direct them as necessary and correct them whenever needed.

Remember, as always, YOU ARE RESPONSIBLE FOR YOUR PRINCIPAL. If something pertaining to security falls through at any venue, it is still your responsibility. With that in mind, you have to let the locals (venue security, production, etc.) know clearly what your needs are. Be aware of possible language barriers that may exist. Some words mean different things in other languages. And, always present your needs as the Principal's needs. They don't know you and really don't care who you are, but when you present yourself with confidence (not arrogance) and tactfully but firmly let them know what the Principal needs, you will usually get better results and more accomplished. And that is the bottom line that the Principal needs to see from you; you get results. If you do not take control of the event, by asking the right questions and making your requests known, they will quickly pick up on it and they will take control. It is unacceptable to allow an outsider to take "control" of your Principal. It is fine and wonderful that they have a plan in place for their event with your Principal, but be sure you tactfully let them know that you will take care of the Principal and anything pertaining to him needs to be run through you. The last thing you need is for your client to come off stage and for eight local guys to crowd around him to "protect him." My first question would be, "If you guys are here, who is watching your original posts where I requested you to be? Hmmmm?" Establish that scenario with the lead security officer during your advance work, so he can pass it along to his team if necessary. Remember, the Principal is going to look to you and wonder why all the officers are here and hold you accountable for this fiasco. It also looks terrible on camera, should they be present. What it really means to the Principal is that you were not proactive in preparing for their function and now you have to react to something that would have been better to just respond to. It is always better to respond than to react. Advanced preparation means everything in this line of work.

Whether at a movie premier, book signing, speaking engagement, concert or interview with the Principal, how you "posture" sets the stage for the crowd. You don't want to stand with a scowl on your face as if you were getting ready to tear someone's head off at a church function. Your posture is very important. How you posture makes a difference and sets the tone in the room.

Interview Stance:

Here's one rule to remember, Wide Base, Deep Base, Low Center, and Head Over Center. Here's the explanation: Your feet should be about shoulder width apart (Wide Base), reactionary "weapon- side" leg should be back a little (Deep Base), your knees should be slightly bent but relaxed (Low Center), and do not lean because a push or pull could easily move you off your base (Head Over Center). Fingers should NEVER be interlocked nor like a military "parade rest." Hands are to be above your waist. The closer the possible threat, the higher your hands should be. Holding the ring finger of the opposite hand gently is a good, natural look, leaning "slightly" forward with chin tucked a little. There is a tendency to lean back, with your head up which causes you to appear to look down your nose at the crowd. That is not a good look. Appear relaxed, but in a position to respond to any situation that may arise, whether it is to grab the Principal and run, move suddenly, or to chop someone in the throat if need be. Be realistic. The other person may be prepared to do the same. Never underestimate your opponent. Trust me... they have already been

"Watching" you...WHILE THEY PREY.

Stage Speaking Engagement

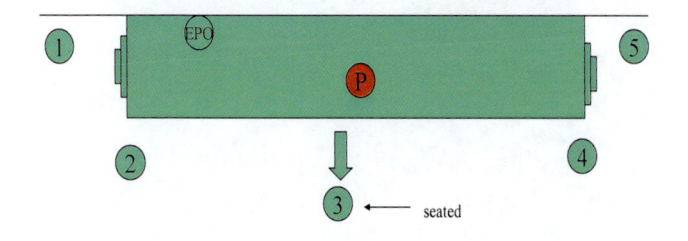

seated

Who is Watching While They Pray | Page 38

Page 39 | Who Is Watching While They Pray

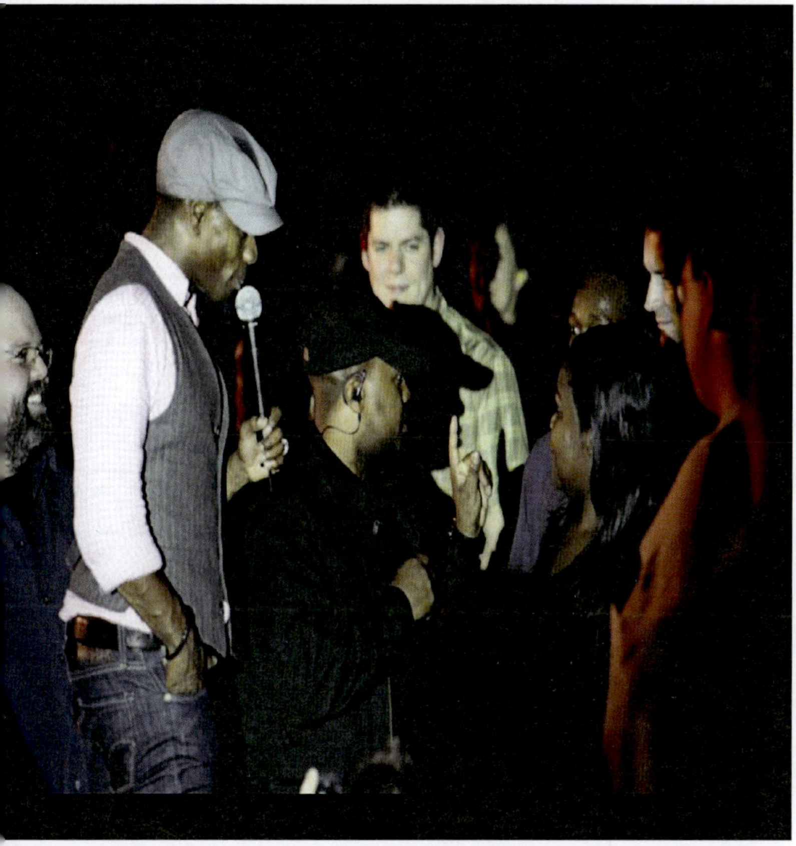

NOTES:

This page intentionally left blank.

CHAPTER SEVEN - Formations

4 Man Diamond Formation

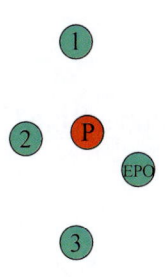

5 Man Hallway Formation

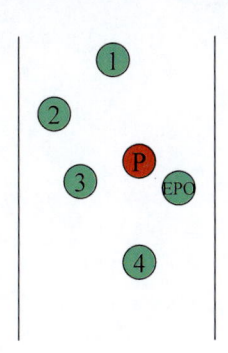

Double Ring Concept

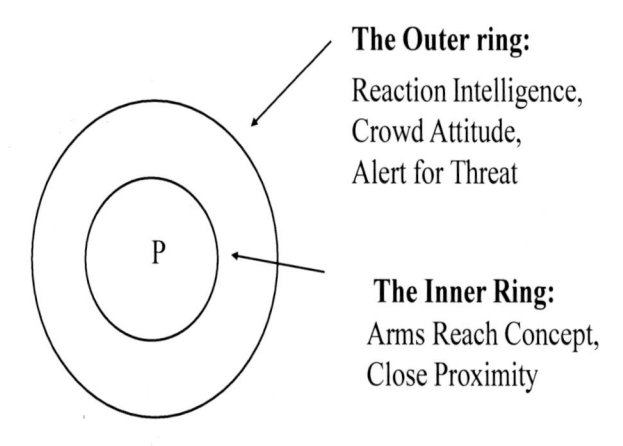

The Outer ring:
Reaction Intelligence,
Crowd Attitude,
Alert for Threat

P

The Inner Ring:
Arms Reach Concept,
Close Proximity

Three Man Triangle Formation

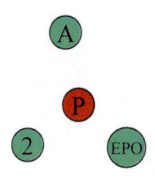

(A)
(P)
(2) (EPO)

Generally used for pastors & mid level dignitaries, etc.

Two Man Formation

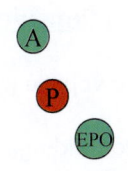

(A)
(P)
(EPO)

Generally used for spouses or low level dignitaries, etc.

There are five primary considerations during an assault:

1. During an assault, protect the principal
2. Arms reach situations (take action if within arm's reach)
3. Take action (cover Principal & respond to threat)
4. Sound off situations (first man who sees problem sounds off)
5. ID problem and use simple terms, ex. gun, knife & location

Cover Considerations:

- Have Principal squat (assist by grabbing belt if needed)
- EPO and Advance Officer close and
- Cover Principal with your bodies facing the threat
- Block item being thrown
- Push the Principal to the ground, if needed, to cover

Emergency Evacuation Considerations:

- Move to vehicle (throw Principal in and cover)
- Move to holding room
- Move to safe location away from problem
- Push the Principal away from the crowd with cover

General Rules:

Protect the right side (if you are right-handed) of the Principal to keep your reactionary (weapon hand) free

Point man should have the Principal in his peripheral view 50% of the time, while keeping his "head on a swivel"

Attempt to block the path of the attacker at all costs

Do not let the Principal enter a doorway first

In hallways keep the Principal in the center

Keep the Principal away from doorways, blind spots, etc.

Move towards the attacker, not away, in case it is a diversion from the threat to get you to go in another direction

Apply pressure to wrist joint and pull up on the thumb to release a hold from a threat or unwanted contact

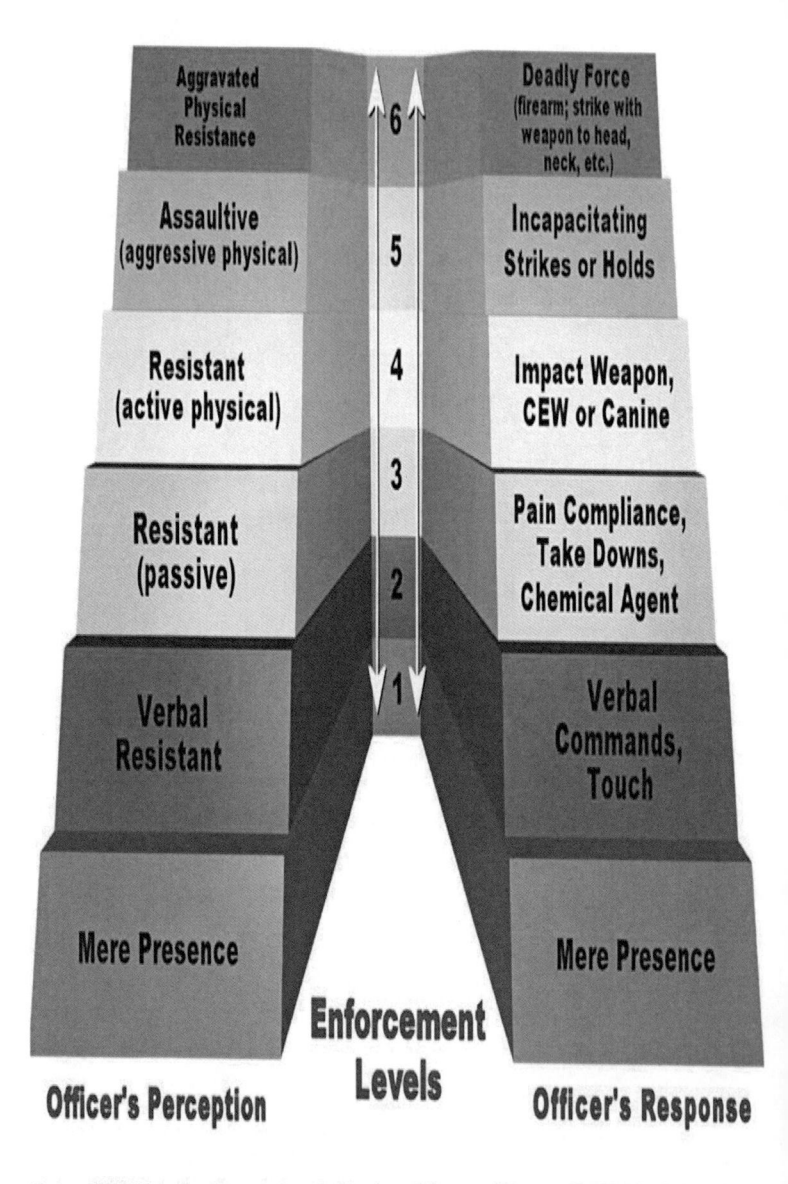

Officer's Perception	Enforcement Levels	Officer's Response
Aggravated Physical Resistance	6	Deadly Force (firearm; strike with weapon to head, neck, etc.)
Assaultive (aggressive physical)	5	Incapacitating Strikes or Holds
Resistant (active physical)	4	Impact Weapon, CEW or Canine
Resistant (passive)	3 / 2	Pain Compliance, Take Downs, Chemical Agent
Verbal Resistant	1	Verbal Commands, Touch
Mere Presence		Mere Presence

Notes: "CEW" is the abbreviation for Conducted Energy Weapon; TASER is the brand of CEW used by both agencies in this study

CHAPTER EIGHT – Guns

The crime reports are in from 2012, and it was a bad year for violence at faith-based organizations. The following are the national numbers, plain and clear:

- There were 135 deadly force incidents discovered (the highest of any year yet). Of those 135 incidents, 39 (28.9%) were an Attack or Assault Resulting in the Death of Others (ARDO's).

- In those 39 ARDOs, 56 victims lost their lives.

- Of those 56 victims, 40 (71.4%) were intentional current or former participants (member, past member, employee, guest, volunteer) of the ministry. Sixteen (16) (such as stories from 12/30, 11/11, 8/16 & 8/7 as examples) were victims of a homicide that took place at the ministry, but had no known victim connection to the ministry.

- Nineteen (19) aggressors (counting suicides) died in these incidents, bringing the total violent deaths at faith-based organizations in 2012 to 75 – the most I have ever seen in one year – by a long way. This was nearly a 39% increase from the previous most violent year (2009) in which we saw 54 violent deaths at FBO's.

- As typical with the multi-year study, nearly 90% of the attackers in 2012 were not stopped by others – they stopped when they were ready to stop. There were only 2 stopped in the process by responding active-duty law enforcement (the Greater Sweet home Missionary Baptist killer on 10/29/12 in Texas, and the Sikh Temple shooter in Wisconsin on 8/5/12). Three (3) were stopped by church members (though one of those was an off-duty officer and one was a former officer).

- The most common weapon was a firearm (55.9%), followed by stabbing weapons (17.9%).

- It was once again evident that the exterior of the buildings is most volatile. Again it was 2:1 more likely that an incident would happen outside than inside.

- **Catholic and Baptist places tied for the most incidents – each had 23 experiences on US soil this year.**

Who was watching while they PREYED? The Unidentified Subject (UnSub), "VIP" or "Signal 13," the would-be criminal looking for that opening or breach in your security layout--this is the one who is looking at you or your team instead of who has the microphone speaking. He never bows his head or closes his eyes during the prayer. He is looking around instead... watching! At offering time, he watches where the money goes from the beginning until it is out of sight. He may even try to go to the restroom at this inopportune time to see if he is hindered in any way. She came in the church last week with a large bible bag to see if you inspected it in the lobby. She tried to see how close to the front of the sanctuary she could sit. He may even get up during the service to take an envelope to the altar or to seemingly pray at the altar to see if security notices in any way. He may follow the little boy to the restroom to see if an adult accompanies them. They may try to use the water faucet on the "children's" side of the church to see if they are redirected or restricted in any way from that area. Someone is yelling out uncontrollably and "everyone" is trying to assist them. So when we all run to that person...Who is Watching the Principal? Unfortunately, sometimes it is someone who intends to do them harm. And they just tested your system to see how easy it would be. Did you pass or fail? It is much better to fail at practice. Lives can be lost if you fail for real. You do not have the luxury of waiting until something happens.

It is too late. Find out why you failed and adjust accordingly, NOW!

Wayne LaPierre, NRA Vice President, recently said after another school shooting, "The only thing that stops a bad guy with a gun is a good guy with a gun." He was pushing for more trained, professional security and protection officers at facilities like schools and churches, where the criminal is usually not expecting to see a gun on the other side.

With the environment constantly changing around us, so is the threat. The threat is dynamic and bounded only by the limits of ingenuity. The point in time at which we install security equipment or implement new security procedures is an imaginary point in time, because it has already passed. The environment has changed. The threat may have changed a little or a lot, but it has changed even if only to deal with whatever you have just put in place. You are being "watched" on every front. While you are thinking of new ways to thwart the would-be criminal, he is thinking of ways around your so-called solutions. Nevertheless, this is not to say it is impossible to be "secure and protected," but to recognize that the process is ongoing. It requires vigilance and dedication, especially if the process is designed to compensate for the changing threat environment.

The first consideration before employing your handgun as an option is to be sure it is the "last resort." Is there another option to get the situation under control? Referencing the Force Continuum chart or Enforcement Levels diagram on the previous page, are there any other options in controlling the immediate threat, like an intermediate weapon or just your hands? The Force Continuum reflects that, depending on the EPO's perception of what the threat is doing, the EPO should respond accordingly to handle the situation. I am not saying that you have to begin at level one on the chart (Presence) and work your way up the chart to level six (Deadly Force). Your professional judgment and mere common sense should guide you up the chart accordingly, and in some cases...you will go straight to level six. Just be sure that when you do, you are mentally and skillfully prepared for what is about to take place.

I heard about a man who got stabbed several times and was lucky to live through the attack because he was so brow-beaten about getting sued and the possibility of prosecution for firing his gun that was already in his hand. His HK P7 remained unfired the entire time he was being stabbed repeatedly. Anyone who would rather be shot, stabbed or injured than in trouble has other issues that need addressing, and that is **not** someone I would want watching my, or my Principal's, back in time of trouble.

Many churches have beefed up their security by adding additional volunteers and even providing EPOs who are dedicated solely to the position of church security. If you are the person directly responsible for the safety and security of the church; are you also the person who is making sure that these individuals are properly screened and trained? What happens when that unfortunate day comes that gun shots are fired within your church or function? You need to establish a clear and precise plan of action for each individual in your protection detail. Everyone cannot run to the Principal and try to save them from the gunman. Someone has to cover the Principal, someone has to look for any additional gunmen, and someone has to contact authorities; oh yeah...and who is addressing the immediate threat by taking out the gunman? You should be the one to design that plan. You should train those officers how you want them to react. You should practice with them and do mock drills on everyone's role. You do not have to let everyone know everything about what you intend to do with the Principal at this time. Only your backup team who assists you in getting the Principal secure should be involved in that conversation.

That is need-to-know information, and honestly, very few need to know. This team of professionals should be highly trained, as you are, and know how to handle their weapons in a crisis. They need also be covered under a licensed security company or be off duty law enforcement. They are covered under some sort of insurance policy while performing their job. This allows for the insurance to fall upon someone other than the church, should the officer do something that may result in a lawsuit.

The bottom line concerning guns in the church is being sure you know who is carrying. Then be sure they are properly trained and licensed to do so. Have a plan in place for use of deadly force. Know the laws, rules and consequences and be sure everyone carrying a weapon does as well. Pray!

IF YOU CARRY A FIREARM, YOU MUST LEARN VERBAL JUDO!

Evaluate the situation by using P.A.C.E.

Problem ^ Audience ^ Constraints ^ Ethical

- Problem
    - What has caused the conflict?
    - Underlying factors?
- Audience
    - Who's involved?
    - Where are they from?
    - Cultural differences, similarities
    - Crowd (What are they seeing?)
    - Are emotions escalating?
- Constraints
    - What barriers do I need to work through?
- Ethical Presence
    - Self-Control (you have the power to take life)
    - Adult EGO State (Adult, Parent, Child)
    - Redirect Negative Behavior

Use the Components of Non-Violent Communication:

- Observe without evaluating
- Express what you are feeling
- Acknowledge what you need
- Make your request clear and concise

Signs of Emotional Distress (Watch Closely):

- Clinched fists
- Rapid breathing
- Sweating
- Red face
- Violent, verbal outburst
- Crying
- Tantrum like behavior
- Body tremors (shaking)
- Stuttering speech
- Intense or fixed eye contact on a target of perceived stress or on your weapon
- "Crazy" eyes

Watch Their Body Language:

- Body does not lie
- Mind controls the body
- What is in a person will come out
- Be ready when it does (proper stance)

NOTES:

Summary-

Learn and know all that you can about your Principal and his business, yet say nothing concerning it to others or them. In this business, you are nothing without your ability to be confidential and discreet. The more you know and say nothing about what you know, the more you can be trusted. And believe me when I tell you...you will be tested on occasion. This line of work is not just about the job, it is about relationship, too. Your job description is not black and white. It is mostly shades of gray. You may step on a few toes at times, but remember, and remind others if necessary, that it is not about you or them for that matter...it is always about the Principal. You have to become a needed, trusted piece of their overall puzzle or you will become expendable. You are more than just a bodyguard. You, my friend, are a highly trained, fast thinking Executive Protection Officer with many skills and integrity beyond reproach. Stay focused out there!

- While I was with them, I protected them and kept them safe and watched over them... John 17:12

Page 59 | Who Is Watching While They Pray

Thank You, HGPS

"Thank you God for surrounding me with people who love this line of work as much as I. Thank you Hairston Global Protective Services (HGPS) for supporting my efforts to keep others safe and secure while operating in what I am ordained to do.

I especially want to thank my brothers, Maurice and Robert Hairston, Deputy Chief Tomisha Spencer, our Guardian Angels Marilyn and James Evans, and my Executive Assistant, Police Officer Brendan Banks for the difficult task in holding down the HGPS Executive Office, my family, and company operations in my frequent absences. If it were not for you guys, I would not be able to flow freely in my anointing and hold it all together. Thank you for believing in me and this book. I love and appreciate you all.

To those I have trained in the past--employees, security volunteers, co-workers, friends, competition, and clients:

Live long, love hard and protect as many as you can while you are here. Make the world know that there was a positive difference in the room because you were there. My brothers and sisters, we are the Watchmen on the Wall. When we fail, many lives are affected. When we succeed, we often go unnoticed. You know, I know and God knows...we make the difference. WE GET IT DONE!"

Curtis Hairston

<u>ABOUT THE AUTHOR</u>

Curtis Hairston is President of Hairston Global Protective Services, Inc. and Hairston Tactical Training Academy based in the Dallas/Fort Worth Metroplex. Hairston is licensed through several State and National Organizations as a Firearms and Tactical Weapons Instructor and an Instructor for Security and Executive Protection Officers. He is an ordained Deacon and currently operates as Executive Director of Security for Bishop T.D. Jakes and The Potters House of Dallas, Inc. He and his company have provided security training and/or protection services for over 50 churches nationwide, and he currently provides security staffing and training at eight local churches in the Dallas/Fort Worth area. He is also the Executive Protection Specialist for Fo Yo Soul Ministries with Minister Kirk Franklin. At the highest level of licensing offered through the Texas Department of Public Safety Private Security Bureau, Hairston has concentrated his gift in preparing today's ministries with a proactive approach on safety and security measures before the incident hits their organization.

WHO IS WATCHING WHILE THEY PRAY?

The Role of Today's Executive Protection Officer

For more information about

WHO IS WATCHING WHILE THEY PRAY?

Seminar scheduling and locations, materials and training aids

and other related services write:

WHO IS WATCHING WHILE THEY PRAY?

4116 S. Carrier Parkway, STE 280-843, Grand Prairie, TX 75052

Or email **info@hairstonprotective.com**

"After 36 years of ministry, I have learned that tragedy doesn't discriminate. One doesn't have to be a Mega church to confront mega challenges. It is my prayer that Curtis Hairston's much needed book will help equip church security to more fully understand the benefit of being well prepared. Mr. Hairston has proven to be an invaluable asset to our organization and many others.

Who is Watching While They Pray, asks a question that every leader must consider. I strongly urge you to allow this textual aid to assist your organization to respond to an ever increasing need that exists in churches today, and more importantly, know what to look for and how to respond, should trouble come!"
-T.D. Jakes Sr., The Potter's House of Dallas

"Being the type of person that doesn't like to bring a lot of attention to myself traveling with security, Curtis Hairston's Executive Protection Team, HGPS, does an excellent job covering myself and my team as we travel across the world, while at the same time blending into the vocabulary of the environment I am in. They make safety and discretion blend with ease."
–Kirk Franklin, Fo Yo Soul Entertainment